An Essex Pastoral

photographs by

Frank Osborne

With a foreword by
Thomas McMahon
Bishop of Brentwood

Ian Henry Publications

© the estate of Frank Osborne
© foreword copyright Thomas McMahon

ISBN 0 86025 511 5

The photograph on the cover is of
the Chelmer at Little Baddow at Easter, 1927

Published by
Ian Henry Publications, Ltd.
20 Park Drive, Romford, Essex RM1 4LH
and printed by
ColourBooks, Ltd.
105 Baldoyle Industrial Estate, Dublin 13, Ireland

FOREWORD

Few people realise that John Betjeman wrote a poem called 'Essex'. I quote the second verse:-

> And as I turn the colour-plates
> Edwardian Essex opens wide,
> Mirrored in ponds and seen through gates,
> Sweet uneventful countryside.

Whilst John Betjeman evokes Essex through the verses of this wonderful poem, Essex of the last century has been captured for us through these photographs. They were taken by Frank Osborne, an early, amateur enthusiast from the village of Old Harlow who cycled around the villages capturing for us these scenes.

Essex is one of the largest counties in the country and in variety of character it must surely take precedence over most of them. From what Dickens used to call 'London over the Border' one moves out to Epping Forest and the mud flats of the estuary of the Thames together with large, flat islands. Parts of Essex are still genuinely rural and there is good farmland, especially around the rolling countryside of Dunmow and up North towards the Stour and Suffolk border. It contains some spectacular villages and fine church and domestic architecture. In accordance with the size and variety of the County is the variety of building materials. In the south-east, walls are most often of Kentish rag; in the east of brown septaria and that curious conglomerate pudding stone; in the north-west of flint and pebble rubble. Knapped flint and flourish work decoration belong of course to the East Anglian border, but go as far south as, for example, St. Osyth. The making of bricks in England seems to have actually started in Essex and probably as early as the 13th century. However, timber for both church towers and porches still remains a feature of some importance, and as for domestic building, timber-framing remained the accepted local technique in spite of the inroads made by brick.

The texts wonderfully complement the photographs and I congratulate Ian Wilkes on both choices of photographs and texts. These photos were left to me quite recently and I hope you will enjoy them as much as I have.

✠ Thomas McMahon
Bishop of Brentwood

KELVEDON HATCH, *1910*

Kelvedon Hatch is a secluded and pleasant place; almost exclusively agricultural, but possessing several good seats. There is no village proper. The largest gathering of houses is about Kelvedon Common and Kelvedon Mill, 1½ miles south of the Church, but these are partly in Doddinghurst parish.

James Thorne - Handbook to the environs of London, 1876

THE WITCH & MOUSE ELM, DODDINGHURST, *1910*

Ingatestone is one of a group of parishes south-west of Chelmsford which all take their name from a tribe called the Gegingas. The use of this word implies a very early Anglo-Saxon settlement in the area. Ingatestone was distinguished form the other - *ing* - names in the area by being Ing-at-Stone, but which stone precisely and what was the significance of the stone, or stones? The name was always in the singular and local tradition explains the stone from which the village took its name as being a Roman milestone. The milestone is variously said to have stood 'near the church' or 'near the village' on the line of the old Watling Street. Whatever it was, the stone was important enough for the inhabitants to name their village after it. If ever there was a Roman milestone it has long since disappeared, but other ancient stones are still extant in the village... The stone at the south door of the church once lay under the north wall. Its present position dates only from the building of the organ chamber in 1905. This makes it highly probable that this stone at least was venerated in pagan times, and then buried beneath the church to emphasise Christianity's power over the old faith.

Stephen Pewsey and Andrew Brooks - East Saxon heritage, 1993

In 1622 Canvey was changed from a semi-morass into dry land when Dutchmen, headed by one called Coppenburgh, built a dyke, or wall, round the island. How well they wrought can be seen today. The island produced crops and became famous for the fattening of cattle. Prosperity arrived, and Saturday nights at the now fairly established 'Lobster Smack' were no doubt something to remember as the monied Dutchmen came in for their pints and sang their boisterous and outlandish songs. Forty-five years later they came again, this time not to construct but to destroy. Landing on the island they harried the people, drove away cattle and set fire to the church. The English fleet openly threatened to join the invaders, a not altogether astonishing circumstance since they were seldom paid. Andrew Marvel in his *Instructions to a Painter*, says,

> Our seamen, whom no dangers shape can fright,
> Unpaid, refuse to mount their ships for spite.
> Or, to their fellows swim on board the Dutch
> Who shew them tempting metal in their clutch.

Archie White - Tideways and byways in Essex and Suffolk, 1948

THE EAGLE INN,
KELVEDON HATCH, *1910*

INGATESTONE HIGH
STREET, *1910*

THE LOBSTER SMACK,
CANVEY ISLAND, *1911*

WICKFORD HIGH STREET, *JUNE, 1912*

AT FOULNESS ISLAND, *JUNE, 1912*

... there is another road to Foulness. The rector writes: "Are you a good walker? From Burnham you walk four miles along the sea-wall, and then look out for a small oyster watch-boat. You shout to the man, and he will put you over for fourpence, unless it is too rough. I have had to sleep on the boat owing to the wind, and my servant once had to do the same owing to fog, but as a rule you can cross. About two miles over fields and ditches will bring you here after landing. I can only promise a warm welcome to atone for a rough journey."

Reginald A Beckett - Romantic Essex, 1901

GREAT WAKERING CHURCH, *EASTER, 1912*

St Nicholas Church has a Norman tower, although it is thought that there might be Saxon origins as it has been documented that a Saxon church stood somewhere in the vicinity. Brian Shannon, Rector of Great Wakering, has created a Friends of St Nicholas Church to take care of the fabric of the building, so that succeeding generations may benefit from it. As the only full-time resident minister in Great Wakering, his activities in the village are too numerous to list. He is school governor of the primary school and involved with Helping Hands and their luncheon club for the elderly. He is Secretary of the Churches Together, which lets all the churches in the village know what the others are doing. Brian is also vicar for Foulness Island where he conducts a Sunday service. He says that although it's quite a small community of people, it is quite distinctive.

Johnnie Quarrell - Portrait of Great Wakering, 1996

Rochford Road, Prittlewell, *1912*

Hockley Road, Rochford, *1912*

Rochford Church, *1912*

Rochford Hall, *1912*

St Andrew. The *pièce de resistance* is the big tall west tower of brick, with diapers of vitrified headers, angle buttresses, a higher south east stair-turret, a big three-light Perpendicular brick window, and battlements. The north side of the church has behind the tower Victorian north aisle and celestory windows, and then the chancel chapel also of red brick, but with two surprising and charming half-timbered gables. The south side was the show side. It has on the aisle and the porch battlements faced with stone and flint chequerwork. The view is dominated by the five-light chancel and the three-light aisle and north chapel windows. The interior has three-bay arcades on octagonal piers with double-chamfered arches. The tower arch is uncommonly tall. The whole is late 15th to early 16th century.

Nikolaus Pevsner - Essex, 1965

It is commonly believed by farm labourers about Rochford where ever May-weed abounds, that those who handle it in weeding the field will suffer from warts. I have often asked, "How is it you have so many warts?" and the answer has been, "They were caused by the May-weed in cleaning such a field," naming one where it was especially common. As a medical man, I should say there is nothing improbable in the theory; the irritation the various forms of May-weed produce may possibly have this effect, and I do know that no man ever hand weeds May-weed without a plentiful crop of these troublesome things afterwards.

Essex Review, v.3, 1894

Rochford Hall ... stands on the edge of a pleasant green, and though lopped and shorn of its former proportions and dignity, is at once recognizable as having been the palatial residence of an ambitious family who have helped to make history. A flat, gabled façade, lighted by many Victorian windows which face out on to the green, and a tall flanking turret still look imposing in that plaster-coated remnant of a fine house. Hardly anything of antiquarian interest exists inside the building, but in the courtyards a few Tudor arches and windows - spared by nineteen-century subverters - yet remain to show what its pristine features were like. The demesne was at one time in the possession of the Boleyn family; but in spite of a persistent tradition to that effect, it seems improbable that Anne, Henry VIII's second queen, was born at Rochford. Anyhow, it is certain that Anne Boleyn could not have first seen the light in the building which at present constitutes Rochford Hall, since all evidence is in favour of the structure being conterminous with the later years of Henry's reign.

Fred Roe - Essex survivals, 1929

The Paglesham smugglers, headed by John Dowsett, emerge as a rather colourful crew in the reminiscences of John Harriott, a Stambridge character who reclaimed Rushley Island with a three mile sea-wall in 1781-2, and, among other many schemes and inventions, originated the Thames river police in 1798. On one occasion he was seeking a passage home from France when it occurred to him that the Paglesham smugglers could take him almost to his doorstep. Harriott was duly deposited within a mile and a half of his home. The gang comprised, in addition to Dowsett, his son-in-law, William Blyth, and two men named Brown and Emberson. Blyth was the local grocer and churchwarden. It is recorded of him that when a bull invaded a field where he was playing cricket he seized the animal by the tail and despite its efforts to escape belaboured it till it died. He himself expired more peacefully in 1830 after reading from the Bible and declaring "Now I am ready for the launch." Unfortunately, before this he had so much confused his ecclesiastical and commercial functions as to use all the Paglesham parish registers for wrapping up butter and bacon.

Hervey Benham - Once upon a tide, 1955

GREAT STAMBRIDGE: LANE TO PAGLESHAM, *AUTUMN, 1924*

PAGLESHAM POST OFFICE, *1914*

THE PLOUGH AND SAIL, PAGLESHAM. *1920*

CANEWDON CHURCH, *JUNE, 1914*

At the head of the Crouch stands a small hamlet called by the significant name of Battlesbridge. Tradition connects this name with the battle of Ashingdon; and it is suggested that a bridge here may have formed the means of escape for the fugitives or the point at which the victors had to give up the pursuit. There is nothing unlikely in the notion that there was a bridge here even in the eleventh century, for the river at this point is very narrow; indeed, this is its highest tidal limit. An iron bridge of one arch spans it today, under which, when I saw it, a thin stream was making its way through an expanse of mud. Below the bridge was a wharf at which a barge with brown sails was moored; above it, a disused water-mill - probably three centuries old - with bare rafters bleaching in the sun and ancient machinery inhabited by rats.

Reginald A Beckett - Romantic Essex, 1901

WOODHAM FERRERS, *JUNE, 1914*

BATTLESBRIDGE, *1914*

In the eleventh and twelfth centuries Maldon was the chief port in Essex and prosperous. Although prosperous still, it is the chief port no longer; no more are 48-gun ships laid down, built and launched as they were three hundred years ago. But shipbuilding goes on in the form of handsome little yachts, and a picturesque working fleet of smacks still lies, when not at work, on the steep, hard riverside. Behind them, tier on tier, buildings of all descriptions pile one upon the other, rising up and up and up to the summit of the hill, where the church of All Saints points to the skies. Of Maldon's many inns, the most interesting from an archælogical point of view is the Blue Boar. Its outward appearance does not prepare one for the sight of the coaching yard surrounded by as fine old timbered buildings of the fifteenth century as one could wish to see.
Archie White - Tideways and byways in Essex and Suffolk, 1948

In the eleventh and twlfth centuries Maldon was the chief port in Essex and prosperous. Although prosperous still, it is the chief port no longer; no more are 48-gun ships laid down, built and launched as they were three hundred years ago. But shipbuilding goes on in the form of handsome little yachts, and a picturesque working fleet of smacks still lies, when not at work, on the steep, hard riverside. Behind them, tier upon tier, buildings of all descriptions pile one upon the other, rising up and up and up to the summit of the hill, where the church of All Saints points to the skies.
Archie White - Tideways and byways in Essex and Suffolk, 1948

Across the fields to the north stands Beeleigh Abbey. The situation is a delightful one, just below a foaming waterfall of the Chelmer, which is crossed by a flat wooden bridge, and formerly turned the wheels of the abbey mill. The Blackwater approaches within a quarter of a mile, and a canal connects the two rivers from which the hamlet of Beeleigh seems to have taken its name. When the abbot and his monks surrendered their river-side dwelling at the Dissolution, it was not pulled down... but the conventual buildings were adapted to the needs of their new owners. Hence the abbey today presents the most delightful jumble of architectural styles, with Early English windows and corbels, groined roofs, buttresses, Tudor fire-places, timbered gables , and clustered chimneys. The church has entirely disappeared, but its site is thought to have been near the old walnut-trees by the river.
Reginald A Beckett - Romantic Essex, 1901

St Mary, Maldon, *Summer, 1920*

Beeleigh Abbey, *1920*

ON LEIGH CLIFFS, *1921*

BENFLEET FROM NEW STATION, *1922*

There is a tradition in Leigh that the original *Mayflower* was built there. It is curious that so little should be known about the origin and fate of the ship that carried the Pilgrim Fathers, so many of whom were Essex men. From time to time correspondence appears in newspapers about it, but nothing conclusive has ever been established about either its first or last days. There were several ships of the same name, and these are sometimes confused. What interests us here is that some of them are known to have been built at Leigh, and it not unlikely that the *Mayflower* we remember was one. But all we know for certain is that its master was a Harwich man.

William Addison - Essex Heyday, 1948

STEEPLE VILLAGE, *1921*

Following the right bank of the estuary you gain from the high ground near Steeple wide views over the marshy valley. Two islands lie in mid-stream - Osea and Northey - each with its single farm, and each connected on the north with the mainland by a rough cart-track practicable only at low water.

Reginald A Beckett - Romantic Essex, 1901

There is no bridge at Hull Bridge, but there is said to be a ferry. When I reached the north bank - on which side there are no houses - the boat was of course upon the further side, where a little street of ancient houses sloped down to the water's edge. I stood on the bank, and shouted "Ferry!" at intervals for nearly half-an-hour. Some men who were hard at work building a large boat ceased knocking; two or three women looked out of their doors, but nothing else happened. Clearly no ferryman was to be expected that day.

Reginald A Beckett - Romantic Essex, 1901

HOCKLEY CHURCH, *1922*

HULLBRIDGE, *EASTER, 1923*

RIVER CROUCH AT HULLBRIDGE, *1923*

A mile of lonely road beyond [Great Wakering] village ends abruptly on the sea-wall at a point known as Wakering Stairs. This seems to be the end of the world; but is it? Not quite. At low tide you may cross the sands to Foulness Island. One of the most curious sights I have ever beheld was when reaching the Stairs just before dusk, there appeared a procession of market-carts rapidly driven across the sands, amid much splashing, through water about a foot deep, with two or three fishing smacks beyond and a distant steamer on the horizon. Having been to Foulness Island before, I did not attempt the journey.

Reginald A Beckett - Romantic Essex, 1901

For a brief period in the 1920 and 1930s, after the new road was opened and before comprehensive military restrictions on access were put in place, Foulness enjoyed an unlikely tourist trade. People drove onto the island from the mainland across to the far seawalls to picnic on the beaches and watch the world go by on the ocean. Tea-rooms and the like were briefly established, but the industry was closed down virtually before it could get going. Some military activities were already in existence at this period - a Sound Raging Laboratory was built at Jerry Wood and a large building project near Courtsend (known as White City) was also embarked upon.

Ian Yearsley - Islands of Essex, 2000

"Access to Foulness in the old days was always across Maplin Sands. If you wanted the doctor, or there was some other emergency, you would have to wait until the tide went out, although it has been known for a doctor to cross from Burnham by boat. That was before the ridge was built, just after the first world war. In the old days the Foulness community was a tightly knit group of mostly farmworkers, often related to each other through marriage or other blood ties. Time has eroded that, although there are families who have their relatives nearby even to this day: this feeling of family is one of the characteristics of the Foulness people, and is often picked up by outsiders."

Johnnie Quarrell - Portrait of Foulness, 1998

The Maplin Sands, *Whitsun, 1923*

The Foulness Road, *Whitsun, 1923*

THE COLNE AT ROWHEDGE, *JUNE, 1925*

RIVER COLNE AT WIVENHOE, *JUNE, 1925*

Rowhedge... dates back to Iron Age Britain in about 5 A.D. The ground was then part of the Iceni fortress of Camulodunum, covering some 12 or 16 square miles, a true fortress city bordered by the Rivers Colne and Roman. It was constructed entirely of wood from the great forests of Essex and was the stronghold of powerful Cunobelin and can be regarded as the capital city of Iron Age Britain... Following the Norman Conquest Rowhedge and East Donulanda seems to have been the property of Queen Maud, wife of King Stephen. Maud was very keen on religious houses and life and eventually swapped East Donulanda with the monks of Colchester's St John's Benedictine Abbey, for land in another area. So the district lived contentedly with the monks as Lords of the Manor for many centuries.
George Pluckwell - Smuggling villages of North East Essex, 1986

Wivenhoe was not a healthy place for smugglers towards the latter end of the eighteenth century, for there was Captain Martin, ruthless in his pursuit of smugglers. His efforts were not sufficient, however, to eradicate the lawbreakers. Opposition seems to whet the spirit of adventure in many people, acting as a challenge rather than a deterrent. The task of the smugglers was facilitated by the co-operation of most of the villagers, from policeman to parson.
Glyn Morgan - The romance of Essex inns, 1964

[Sabine] Baring-Gould gives a lively, though all too brief, glimpse of Wivenhoe during regatta time. The description of Mr Charles Pettican's residence, with *Medusa*'s figurehead and the mast on the lawn, is excellent: the wooden house with its emerald green shutters and gilded balcony, and the tiled roof which 'looked very red, as though red ochred every morning by the housemaid after she had pipeclayed the walls.' Various houses have been suggested as the original of the old shipbuilder's residence, but the author of *Mehalah* probably only described a type of abode which is very usual in such riverside settlements as Wivenhoe.
Fred Roe - Essex survivals, 1929

The normal travelling time [on the Chelmer & Blackwater Navigation] from Heybridge Basin to Springfield Basin was about 12 hours - a long, tiring day for a two-man crew. They took turns leading the horse and steering, so there was no chance for a rest. It became usual for the Heybridge men to bring a loaded barge to Paper Mill [lock] and exchange it for an empty one from Chelmsford. In this way both crews could return to base every evening.

John Marriage - Barging into Chelmsford, 1997

PAPER MILL LOCK, LITTLE BADDOW, *1926*

EASTWOOD LANE, *AUTUMN, 1926*

COCKTHEHURST, EASTWOOD, *EASTER, 1927*

TOLLESBURY, *EASTER, 1927*

THE GRIFFIN, DANBURY, *EASTER, 1927*

Once a large fishing village, Tollesbury now offers acres of lonely saltings and sea walks where birds can be watched against vast, ever-changing skyscapes.

Stan Jarvis - Essex, 1997

At Danbury, one of the most beautifully situated villages in Essex, some 380 feet above the sea level, is the Griffin Inn, a picturesque, gabled structure, dating from Elizabethan times, but much pulled about in later years. Situated midway between Chelmsford and Maldon the Griffin makes a very convenient house of call and is deservedly popular. At the time of writing the process of unpicking its half-timbered front has been partially carried out, and the whole building, after many years of injudicious plastering, is now beginning to assume something of its ancient aspect. It lies immediately facing the pathway to the church on the breezy summit of the hill; close by is the old smithy, and, on the opposite side of the road a range of early sixteenth-century tenements. A pleasant dining-room of large size with a beamed ceiling occupies the ground floor of the west wing of the inn, and from this a doorway opens out on to an old-world garden. In the quaint entrance bar some fragments of Perpendicular carving, waifs from the church screen, have been fitted... As is the case with so many of our ancient hostelries, very little is actually known of the history of the Griffin Inn, but for generations past it has aroused interest. At the commencement of the nineteenth century Joseph Strutt, the antiquary, wrote a regular Wardour Street romance entitled *Queenhoo Hall* ... many of the scenes of this forgotten novel were laid at the Griffin... Its author died in 1802 leaving the romance unfinished. More high-falutin nonsense in literature it would be difficult to find, and such indeed was the opinion of a rising young man who was asked by the publishers to complete the work for them. *Queenhoo Hall* was produced in 1808, with Scott's two chapters in conclusion.

Fred Roe - Essex Survivals, 1929

BELL INN AND CHURCH, PURLEIGH,
JUNE, 1927

... The first glimpse of Purleigh, a glimpse such as one feels would be a rich reward for the weariest day's tramping. There is a stretch of common, bordered by a few cottages on the left, while on the right rises the smoke from a dusky encampment of gipsies, whose lean horses stray in search of pasture.

Reginald A Beckett - Romantic Essex, 1901

PURLEIGH STREET, *JUNE, 1927*

BEHIND THE BELL, PURLEIGH, *JUNE, 1927*

Lawrence Washington of Purleigh, ejected minister; great-great-grandfather of George Washington, President of the United States of America; fellow of Brasenose College, Oxford; rector of Purleigh, 1632-43; ejected by Puritans, probably because the living was too valuable to be enjoyed by one who was not of their party. His son, John, who settled in Virginia, 1656, was joined later by his brother, Lawrence. John was the father of Lawrence, the father of Augustine, the father of George.

William Addison - Essex Heyday, 1949

Mundon is almost a forgotten parish in the Dengie Hundred, three miles south of Maldon, on a creek of the River Blackwater. The church, dedicated to the Virgin Mary, sits alone beside Mundon Hall. Morant described the church as "... tyled and so is the chancel. The Belfry is framed of timber and plastered, octangular below above four square boarded and tyled. In it are three bells." In the 1830s Wright described it simply as "a small ancient building, dedicated to the Virgin Mary." St Mary's is often described as a 'beautiful little church' which it is. It undoubtedly has Norman foundations - built within the moat of Mundon Hall. The building you see today was built of rubble (now coated with plaster) in the 14th century. The chancel was rebuilt early in the 18th century, is 20 by 16 feet, and retains its original east and north windows. The nave... houses, in the north wall, an early 14th century window with Y-tracery and a blocked doorway. On the south is a blocked doorway of the 18th century and, further east, a fine Tudor brick window appears. A blocked 16th century archway led to a now demolished chapel. The wonderful timber north porch has been dated to about 1600 and was described by Hewett as "the finest example of its kind seen in the county". The characteristic hexagonal timber belfry is by far the most well known part of the church.

Andrew Barham - Lost parish churches of Essex, 2000

MUNDON HALL, *JUNE, 1927*

MUNDON CHURCH, *JUNE, 1927*

SALCOTT CHURCH, *EASTER, 1927*

In *Mehalah*, [Sabine] Baring-Gould, who was rector of East Mersea for ten years, writes [that] Salcott and Virley are believed to have been notorious haunts of smugglers, and Baring-Gould was probably recording fact when he said that the 'nots' in the decalogue on the wall of the church at Salcott, where the church itself is said to have been used for storing smuggled goods, had all been erased. There can be no doubt that they had been erased from the consciences of the villagers.

William Addison - Essex Heyday, 1949

THE BELL, WOODHAM WALTER, *JUNE, 1927*

WOODHAM WALTER, *JUNE, 1927*

TERLING, *JUNE, 1927*

..IINGFIELD, *1929*

The local people pronounce the name to rhyme with 'darling'. The river Ter runs deep in it bed, splashing into a wide pool below the village. From there the rise into the village from the south-west is one of the most satisfactory approaches to any Essex village. Across the green the red-brick tower of All Saints' church has an unusual sundial high up on its wall. Terling Place has been the home of the Strutt family since it was built around 1765. John William Strutt, third Baron Rayleigh (1842-1919) won the Nobel prize doe physics in 1904. The family still owns much of the village, whose pink and white plastered cottages make it popular with photographers.

Stan Jarvis - Essex, 1997

The minutes of a parish meeting in Finchingfield:
At the meetinge at Gyles Wolfes this 24th of February, 1630.
Imprimis it is agreed that goodman Chaplyn, goodman Wolfe, and goodman Chote shal goe to Waldone to bye some Corne for the poore.
It is agreed that Edward Johnsone shall have somethinge allowed him for a while vntil it please God his wife recover her health.
It is agreed that Murgan should carry a letter to Mr Wallis about some Corne. He is to be allowed xvi d. for his Jurnye.
It is agreed that Watsone should kepe Garrettes child a while should be allowed 20d. by the week for kepinge of it, afterwarde that it should be putt out a Sume of monye is to be given with it.
It is agreed that Mr Brouen, Mr Sparrow, Mr Tyme, Richard Harrington, Thomas Whithead, Will Moswell and Simon Wyborowe should be spoken to for to Joyne with us in our Monthly Meetinge.

Essex Review, vol. viii, p.128

The Abbey was founded by King Stephen about 1140 and made Cistercian in 1148. Of the C12 church no traces remain above ground. Of the cloisters of it a little has recently been excavated: typical mid C12 stone capitals and bases and a slender shaft with spiral grooves and nail-head projections. As regards the monastic buildings there are indications of the dormitory undercroft. This must date from c.1180, but the vaulting is an early C13 addition. A fine C13 doorway leads from the dormitory into a completely preserved corridor. This is two-storeyed and has single-chamfered ribs and arches to the E. The details of the vaulting are again early C13. s of the corridor and of the dormitory range the Abbot's Lodging. It has lancet windows with round heads inside. The same windows also in a detached building SE of the former. This is not aligned with the dormitory and cloister. From its style and from documentary evidence Mr S Gardner attributes these two buildings to c.1185-90. Finally, completely detached from all the rest the chapel of St Nicholas, the gate chapel or capella extra porters of the abbey - a plain rectangle with lancet windows, on the N side quite regularly arranged. The date must be about 1225. In this and all the other buildings the most remarkable feature is the extensive use of brick dressings - and brick which is definitely not Roman. It is very early, as medieval brickwork goes in England. After the Dissolution a house was built into the abbey premises. It lies N of the corridor and has a porch, an original hall, and a fine N chimneystack. A date 1581 was on the porch. Inside a good screen with Doric pilasters, C17 panelling, etc. In one room is a circular C12 Pier. The picture at the back of the house with the C16 and the medieval buildings, the fast-flowing mill stream, and a weatherboarded mill is of great charm.

Nikolaus Pevsner, Essex, 1965

COGGESHALL ABBEY, *1929*

At length Sigbert reigned in Essex; he became a Christian, and took to him a holy man named Cedde, or Chadde, who won many, by preaching and good life, to the Christian religion. Cedde, or Chad, was by Finan consecrated Bishop of the East Saxons, and he ordered priests and deacons in all the parts of Essex, but especially at Ithancaster and Tilburie. This city of Ithancaster (saith Ralph Cogshall) stood on the banks of the river Pante, that runneth by Maldun, in the hundred an Danesey, but is now drowned in Pante, so that nothing remaineth, but in the ruin of the city in the river.

John Stow - The Chronicles of England, 1580

St-Peter-on-the-wall stands astride the west wall of the Roman fort [of Othona]. It is in all probability the very church built by St Cedd, c.654. It consists of nothing but the nave, but the existence of a west porch and an apsed chancel as wide as the nave have been ascertained.

Nikolaus Pevsner - Essex, 1965

St Nicholas. The nave north doorway is Norman. Fine Early English chancel with three stepped east lancets and a quatrefoil above and single lancets on the north and south sides - all renewed outside. The plain sedilia and piscina also belong to the C13. C14 south arcade of four bays with octagonal piers and double-chamfered arches, renewed probably when the south aisle was rebuilt in 1866. The chancel arch of the same style. The west tower is also C14, with angle buttresses and west window of two cusped lights with pointed quatrefoil in the spandrel. The battlements are later. Font late Norman, with plain square bowl on quatrefoil foot with attached angle shafts. Carved foliage. Brass to Edward Wiot, d.1584, kneeling figure.

Nice village street widening just south of church into a Green. Many weatherboarded cottages. A number of these were erected as late as 1881 by the Dean and Chapter of St Paul's, who are lords of the manor.

Nikolaus Pevsner, Essex, 1965

St Peter on the Wall, Ithancaster, *1929*

Tillingham, *1929*

HAZELEIGH HALL, *1930*

The little church of St Nicholas, Hazeleigh, lay two and a half miles southwest of Maldon, next to the Old Hall. It has the dubious distinction of having often been quoted as 'the meanest church in Essex'. Made of lath and plaster over a timber frame it is thought to have been built by Giles Aleyne and his wife Sarah in about 1600. However, some authors have suggested that the chancel was built earlier while others believe the nave was built a century later. It is thought, by most historians, to have incorporated timbers from an earlier structure on the same site. The first rector was installed in 1390 before which Hazeleigh was only a chapel, perhaps attached to Woodham Mortimer Church. Hazeleigh parish registers date from 1575.

Andrew Barham, Lost parish churches of Essex, 2000

Essex has always grown apples, apples of repute and fine flavour. Some say the Essex Cox surpasses all others; certainly no pippin can compare with the D'Arcy Spice, whose rough coat hides the sweetest heart. Born and bred in an Essex orchard, this centuries old apple, they say, can only reach maturity on Essex soil. Today apple growing is a major industry. Highly technical, highly skilled, Essex fruit growers employ a factory technique in the production of their crops. But whatever the form of culture, whatever the method of pest and disease control, whatever the means of storage and packing, apples must be picked by hand, and by Essex hands which from long use have acquired a gentle touch.

Stuart Rose - An Essex dozen, 1953

TOLLESHUNT D'ARCY, *1930*

HIGH EASTER, *1932*

In the days when village postmasters franked their own post many collectors of postmarks travelled here specially to obtain these unusual specimens. 'Easter' comes from the Old English 'estre', a sheepfold.
Stan Jarvis - Essex, 1997

The approach to the church from the village is charming, a narrow passage between two 15th century timber-framed and gabled houses. Others opposite.
Nikolaus Pevsner - Essex, 1965

COGGESHALL, *1935*

Paycocke's house is full of relics of the cloth industry. The merchant mark of the Paycockes, an ermine tail, looking like a two-stemmed clover leaf, is to be found on the carved beams of the chimney, on the breastsummers of the fireplaces, and set in the midst of the carving along the front of the house. Thomas marked his bales of cloth thus, and what other armorial bearings did he need? His house stood in West Street, opposite the vicarage, and was the delight of all who saw it. It stands there still, and looking upon it today and thinking of Thomas Paycocke who once dwelt in it, do there not come to mind the famous words of Ecclesiasticus?
Let us now praise famous men and our fathers that begat us.
The Lord hath wrought great glory by them through His great power from the beginning...
Rich men furnished with ability, living peaceably in the habitations:
All these were honoured in their generations and were the glory of their times.

Eileen Power - Medieval people, 1924

Pleshey is a very good example of those numerous places which were formerly of great importance, but are now (save historically) of no importance whatever. The general aspect of Pleshey, with the castle-mound dominating the village which winds round its base, is striking reminiscent of feudal times. But it has even deeper roots in the past. Its earliest name was Tumbelstoun, or Town of the Tumuli, showing it to have been inhabited by the ancient Britons. There are many signs of this, of which it will be sufficient to mention the outer embankment and ditch, enclosing the entire village within its circular span in the space of about forty acres. When the Romans invaded the country, they could not leave so strong a place in the hands of the conquered race, and would necessarily take possession of it themselves: that they actually did so is proved by the fragments of Roman pottery and tiles which have been dug up. It is probable, but not certain, that in later centuries this stronghold was occupied by the Danes. But from the time of the Conquest we find it definitely the seat of the High Constables of England, in whose keeping it remained for about four hundred years.

Reginald A Beckett - Romantic Essex, 1908

Bid him, - O, what?
With all good speed at Plashy visit me.
Alack, and what shall good old York there see
But empty lodgings and unfurnish'd walls,
Unpeopled offices, untrodden stones?

William Shakespeare - Richard II

Once there were three Wendens: Wenden Lofts, Great Wenden and Little Wenden. The parish church of Little Wenden was situated 'on the left side of the road from Wenden Lofts to Great Wenden'. Its dedication is unknown. The only reference I have been able to find describing its appearance is in an old will which mentions the church as having a tower. The churches of Little Wenden and Great Wenden were less than a mile apart and the joint population was not large enough to keep up payments for both churches. Therefore, at the request of the parishioners, and with the consent of the Earl of Suffolk (patron of both churches), the parishes of Great and Little Wenden were united in 1662 by Bishop Sheldon. Great Wenden then became known as Wendens Ambo. Little Wenden's church and Great Wenden's vicarage, both being ruinous, were pulled down.

Andrew Barham - Lost parish churches of Essex, 2000

PLESHEY, *1932*

WENDENS AMBO, *1933*

HARLOW LOCK, *OCTOBER, 1936*

HARLOW MILL, *OCTOBER, 1936*

HATFIELD FOREST, *1935*

COGGESHALL PRIORY, *28 MARCH, 1937*

HARLOWBURY CHAPEL, *DECEMBER, 1935*

Harlowbury chapel dates from c.1180, and was probably the private chapel of the manor. It is a small, rectangular building, of flint rubble with stone dressings and later brick buttresses. The north doorway, with semi-circular arch and carved waterleaf capitals, is original, as are round-headed windows in the north, east and south walls. The walls were heightened and the roof renewed in the 15th century. In the 17th century an upper floor was inserted when the building was adapted for agricultural use.

Victoria History of the County of Essex, volume VIII, 1983

Gaston Green, *2 November, 1937*

The edge of the wood, Carter's Green, *14 November, 1937*

As labourers' cottages were not large enough to hold all the guests invited to a wedding, there was often a large room in the parish, conveniently near the church, kept for the purpose. Only one of these is left. It is the fifteenth-century Marriage Feast Room at Matching. It was always the custom at village jollifications, and particularly at wedding banquets, to bring food as well as gifts for the home, so that 'the more the merrier' was a fact. No labourer in the old days could have borne the expense of providing for so many as usually came. It was therefore understood that he should only be at the charge of bread and beer.

William Addison - Essex Heyday, 1949

MATCHING, CHURCH AND MARRIAGE FEAST ROOM, *14 NOVEMBER, 1937*

The church makes an extremely pleasing picture with Matching Hall, its barn and dove-cote, the pond with a brick fishing hut, and the Rectory on the other side.

Nikolaus Pevsner - Essex, 1965

MATCHING CHURCH, *14 NOVEMBER, 1937*

MATCHING HALL, *14 NOVEMBER, 1937*

On New Year's Day, 1641, the bell-ringers of Latton played a prank that brought several of them before the justices assembled at Chelmsford for the Epiphany sessions. John Starkys of Latton, servant to Mr Den, the parson, gave information that 'two of the sayde ringers, namelye, Jeremye Reeve, servant to William Stracye of Latton aforesayde, and William Skinner, sonne to Widow Skinner of the sayde towne, did from the belfreye repaire to the Communion table in the Chancell of the sayde Church, and in the sight of this Informant, as hee was standing in the bellfreye, pull down the rales from about the sayde Table with theire bare hands. And sayeth that hee this Informant goeing out into the Churchyard did see the sayde Reeve and Skinner together with Henrye Wennell, apprentice to John Starkys of the sayde Latton Potter, and one Henrye Vinton, servant to one, Poole, a dish turner of the same, bringing the sayde rales out of the Chancell into the Churchyard and from thence throwe them over the Churchyard wall into the Higheway. And hee further sayeth that hee did see the sayde persons carrye the sayde broken rales neare to the whipping post of that towne, and there set them on fire.'

John Case, servant to James Altham of Mark Hill, said that John Wright, a carpenter of Latton Potter, was also 'at the drinkeing of the sayde beer, and payed for part thereof, and that theye did send for it to releeve theire necessitie.' In the course of a lengthy examination of four bell-ringers 'touching a supposed riotous misdemeanour done by them in Latton Church' on this occasion it cam out in the evidence of William Skynner that the ringers 'did laye their moneyes together to the summe of two shillings, and sent Wennell for beere. And the sayde Wennell brought a Kilderkin, or such like vessell of beere, for the sayde moneye from the Black Lyon, an alehouse in Harlowe, on his shoulders, and sett it downe neare the Highe waye, where the rales were fired. And hee, the sayde Skynner, further sayeth that the sayde vessell was carryed thence (but hee knoweth not by whome) into the sayde Church porch, where the greater part of the sayde beere was dranke by them, the other Examinats, and divers others.'

William Addison - Essex Heyday, 1948

THE COMIC COTTAGE OF LATTON, *27 FEBRUARY, 1938*

MARK HALL, *3 SEPTEMBER, 1937*

MARK HALL PARK, *21 NOVEMBER, 1937*

THE GREYHOUND, NETTESWELL, *20 APRIL, 1940*

Turning westward, I followed a beautiful road, overlooking the valley of the Stort to Netteswell Cross. This little hamlet stands, as its name suggests, at the junction of intersecting roads; its exquisite Greyhound Inn and quaint cottages are charmingly grouped in a little green hollow, and should be a godsend to a painter in search of a subject.

Reginald A Beckett - Romantic Essex, 1901

Mark Hall Gardens, Muskham Road, Harlow. Three walled gardens are devoted to unusual fruits, a garden in the seventeenth-century style with the parterre effect then so fashionable, and, in the largest of the three, a demonstration of a variety of gardening styles and techniques.

Stan Jarvis - Essex, 1997

The Vicarage, Harlow, *28 January, 1940*

St Mary's Schools, Harlow, *21 February, 1939*

MORETON, *2 AUGUST, 1939*

Moreton, a very compact little hamlet, clusters around the junction of two roads presenting a quiet unpretentious picture with its huddle os buildings, weatherboarded, or cream and white-washed, with their roofs predominately mellow tiled, the whole pleasingly varied by trees and gardens. Moreton's small thirteen century church, its tower built in 1787, has no fewer than seven lancet windows lighting its tiny chancel. A village has been here for centuries and I discovered that its early Lords of the Manor paid the king this seemingly extraordinary payment for the pleasure of owning Moreton... one man with a horse valued at ten shillings, four horseshoes, a leather sack and one iron fastening whenever his royal master should go into Wales.

W R Finch - Journeying into Essex, c.1950

Thaxted (the thatched placed) is a town which has contributed no striking event to our history; there is no particular spot in it hallowed by national association; and yet the whole aspect of the place is eloquent of the past. It seems to have been the Sheffield of the Middle Ages, before coal had taken the place of wood as fuel. The timber of the weald country around it glowed in its furnaces, wherein were tempered the most famous knives and swords; one of its outlying hamlets is still called Cutler's Green. As you enter the town from the south, the first buildings you note in the broad street are great thatched barns or warehouses standing closed and empty. As you proceed past silent houses and shop, the road divides, and at the corner stands the old Moot Hall, with overhanging upper storeys raised on stout oaken pillars. Here still hang two poles with large iron hooks, formerly used for pulling the thatch from burning houses.

Reginald A Beckett - Romantic Essex, 1901

Thaxted became one of the major venues of Morris dancers largely due to the enthusiasm of the remarkable Conrad Noël, one-time pastor of the town's glorious church. If he was the inspiration - then his wife was the person who transformed his ideas into reality. When they first arrived in the town, one dance - the Broom Dance - was still being performed occasionally in the Carpenters' Arms (alas! no longer a pub). The old bell that was a feature of this particular dance was given to Mrs Noël by the scion of the dancing family who had treasured it for generations. Perhaps it was this gift that inspired her to assemble a team of young people who shared her interest. Whatever the reason, they were soon footing it neatly to the traditional dances - Bean Setting, Rigs o'Marlow, and How d'ye do, Sir?

Glyn Morgan - Secret Essex, 1982

THE MOOT HALL, THAXTED, *25 MARCH, 1940*

THAXTED, EASTER MONDAY, *25 MARCH, 1940*

LITTLE HALLINGBURY CHURCH, *31 AUGUST, 1940*

St Mary the Virgin. Norman south doorway with Roman bricks C13 chancel with renewed lancet windows. Belfry half-timbered with recessed shingled spire. Interesting south porch of timber with unusual tracery of squashed ogee arches and squashed circles with ogee tops and bottoms - C14. Pretty group north-west of the church of timber-framed house with symmetrical outer gables, weatherboarded barn, and brick maltings behind a little pond.

Nikolaus Pevsner - Essex, 1965

SHEERING MILL, *28 JULY, 1940*

LITTLE PARNDON FROM THE MILL, *28 APRIL, 1940*

UGLEY GREEN, *3 MAY, 1940*

ELSENHAM, *3 MAY, 1940*

The people of Ugley, however sensitive they are as to its name, must agree that it has given their village some degree of prominence. To see it in print is to wish to pay it a visit. The list of vicars in the church is headed 'Oakley', but the *Book of Essex Place Names* says authoritatively and with rather unkind emphasis 'Oakley is a modern euphemism for which there is no etymological justification.' It gives several variations including Uggheleam (1086), Hog(e)le (1284), but the nearest to Oakley is Ukeley (1535). It appears that in far off days a certain Ucga made the first clearing in the forest, hence 'Ucga's clearing' or 'Ucga's ley'. So you see it is just bad luck for a pretty place that his should not have been a pretty name and that he should have given it to his settlement.

W R Finch - Journeying into Essex, c.1950

The 5½ mile long Elsenham & Thaxted Light Railway was promoted by local interests to save Thaxted from further decline for lack of a railway (population had fallen from 2,556 to 1,650 between 1851 and 1901) and to assist badly depressed local agriculture. Receiving financial help from the Great Eastern Railway and the Treasury, the line was sanctioned in 1906, begun in 1911 and opened under GER operation on 1 April, 1913. The five or so daily services, mostly mixed and carrying a tow rope for shunting at Sibleys, the one proper station (there were also three halts), were at first well patronised, but a 25 mph restriction, the anachronistic six-wheeled coaches with end-steps (replaced by corridor stock only in 1948) and the need for rebooking at Elsenham left the branch helpless before road competition. Passenger facilities were withdrawn on 15 September, 1952, the freight services on 1 June, 1953, since when almost all traces of the line have disappeared.

D I Gordon - The Eastern Counties (A Regional History of the Railways of Great Britain), 1968

St Mary. Quite a big building, all of 1864, except for the north transept and north wall. Sumptuous screen for Essex, with large one-light divisions. dado panels with quatrefoil frieze at the foot, blank tracery, and two top friezes. Cusped and crocketed ogee arches are the main motif above, surmounted by panel tracery. Broad straight cornice.

Manuden Hall, north-east of the church. Much altered, but of the original mid 16th century house there remain the two south gables of the west front, stepped with pinnacles on the two apexes. The windows below may also be original. on the ground floor mullioned and transomed, on the upper floor only mullioned. All the individual lights are arched.

Manuden has a specially pretty, short village street with timber-framed cottages with oversailing upper floors neat the church and a small assortment of Georgian houses and little further west.

Nikolaus Pevsner - Essex, 1965

THE END OF ALBA WOOD, ELSENHAM, *3 MAY, 1940*

MANUDEN CHURCH, *OCTOBER, 1940*

MANUDEN STREET, *OCTOBER, 1940*

St Mary the Virgin. 1859 by Joseph Clarke.
Hassobury. 1868 by the younger Hardwick. A large grey Tudor mansion with gables, asymmetrically composed.

Nikolaus Pevsner - Essex, 1965

HASSOBURY FROM FARNHAM CHURCHYARD, *OCTOBER, 1940*

FARNHAM CHURCH FROM EAST, *OCTOBER, 1940*

The Forest of Hatfield is an old deer park which once formed part of the estates of the Houblons of Hailingbury Place. It is all that remains of a once extensive Royal Hunting Ground - part of the great Forest of Essex. In the early 1920s the Hailingbury Estate was broken up and concern was expressed at the felling of a great number of fine trees. Thanks to the generosity of the Buxton family and later benefactors the forest was saved and presented to the National Trust. It now comprises over one thousand acres of woodland: fewer large trees than of yore but with coppices of oak and hornbeam and many fine maples with scattered stands of silver birch. Armed with a pocket-size book on tree identification, the visitor will find specimens of many other of our native trees: alder, black poplar, elm, Horse chestnut, etc., and much thorn (often sporting a mistletoe bough). Needless to say, there is a wealth of flora and fauna.

William A Bagley - Walks for motorists - Essex, 1982

CATTLE IN HATFIELD FOREST, *8 SEPTEMBER, 1950*

You must go to Thaxted in Essex. Here you will behold a very small and ancient town, with a Guildhall of half-timbered work, overlooking a broad square, and you will walk up a cobblestone street, past a quaint jumble of houses, one of which is popularly supposed to have been the abode of Dick Turpin, to the Church of Our Lady, St John Baptist, and St Lawrence. The church is a wonderful pile, chiefly of fifteenth-century work. From without it is beautiful and expressive, but not more so than many a similar building of old England. The great wonder of the church is the interior. To the visitor who enters it for the first time, it seems that a great orchestra has burst out into glorious harmony. Without doubt it is the most beautiful church in the world! You may smile at my enthusiasm, but you have not seen it. If you have music in your soul, and thus are not fitted for stratagems or blinded by prejudice, you will, I think, agree with me. There is nothing in the church that is expensive. There is nothing that could not be fashioned in almost any church. A good deal of the work is evidently done by the people of the place, untrammelled by the tyranny of church furnishers. The hangings and tapestry are woven by hand, and in the simplest way; yet the effect is an overpowering one of the joy of living, the beauty of goodness, and of the love of Him Who came that we might have life and have it more abundantly.

Donald Maxwell - A detective in Essex, 1933

Thaxted Church contains some noticeable oak fittings, among them a font cover and case which completely enclose the baptismal vessel. This elaborate structure, which towers up to a great height, is crocketed and displays traceried arches in panels of late fifteen-century design. It may be added that the gargoyles which serve on Thaxted Church comprise some of the most hideous chimeras ever invented by medieval sculptors.

Fred Roe - Essex Survivals, 1929

THAXTED MOOT HALL, *AUGUST, 1952*

GARGOYLES, THAXTED, *AUGUST, 1952*

FROM SOUTH-WEST DOOR OF THAXTED CHURCH, *1952*

SAFFRON WALDEN, *23 MARCH, 1940*

In the year 1252 a famous tournament was held at Walden, at which a knight, Sir Ernauld de Mounteney, was slain by Sir Roger de Leeburn, not without some suspicion of foul play. It was not until the reign of Edward III that the additional name of Saffron was given to the town, a name which still remains, though the saffron plant is no longer cultivated in the neighbourhood.

C R B Barrett - Essex, 1892

Saffron is perhaps the most famous of all the Essex herbs, having given its name to Saffron Walden. Saffron is a small plant, much like a crocus, which flowers in the autumn. It has bright orange stigmas which are collected to make a bright yellow dyestuff and flavouring. Scores of women and girls used to work in the fields gathering the stigmas by hand, but as it took between 60,000 and 192,000 stigmas to make one pound of saffron, it was a very backbreaking task.

Lynn Pewsey - A taste of Essex, 1994

"When I was eleven I went to Friends' School, as a day girl. There were very few day pupils there in those days, but I enjoyed it, the games were the part that I liked the most. We were very disciplined there and if you were naughty you were kept in, which was unfair because we worked Saturday mornings and I had a half holiday on Wednesdays. I used to get punished at home, or told off at home as well as at school, because I couldn't hide the fact that I had to go back to school. None of the day girls stayed for lunch. After we'd had games in the afternoon, which were two or three times a week and a match on Saturdays, then we could wear what we liked.

"There were all the basic lessons and there was chemistry and languages. I did French and Latin. They weren't taught very well in those days and there was such an anti-German feeling that my father would not let me learn German, which was an awful pity. There was great emphasis on games and we used to have gym and swimming, they had a swimming bath. It was a terrific asset, wonderful. The swim-suits were very 'allover'! But of course it was a mixed school and we were only separated for needlework, swimming and gym. Funnily enough, we did carpentry there, which I loved, having been brought up with big brothers, there was a workshop at home, you see. I was much better at that side of it than I was on the academic. Despite the girls being included in carpentry, the boys were not expected to do needlework. Being a boarding school, one session was for mending, and they had to do it again properly: it wasn't right. but of course we had black woollen stockings, you could image! The poor boarders did really suffer badly."

Gillian Holman - Violet Dix's Trunk, 1996

SAFFRON WALDEN
HIGH STREET,
1954

FRIENDS' SCHOOL,
SAFFRON WALDEN,
AUGUST, 1954

ST MARY'S, HARLOW, *21 FEBRUARY, 1939*

Alas so thoroughly restored in 1878-80 that it is virtually a Victorian church. Only the fact of a crossing tower remains as evidence that Harlow belonged to that type very unusual in Essex. Between the medieval church and the present rebuilding lay another rebuilding of 1709.

Nikolaus Pevsner - Essex, 1965

Dorrington Hall, Sheering, opposite Aylmers. Built c.1770. Five-bay front perhaps altered and originally of seven bays. Centre with pediment and Corinthian porch. Bay windows to the left and right above them Venetian windows.

Nikolaus Pevsner - Essex, 1965

HIGH STREET, HARLOW, *AUTUMN, 1955*

DURRINGTON HALL, *2 OCTOBER, 1957*

Battlesbridge 13
Beeleigh 15
Benfleet 16
Canewdon 12
Canvey Island 3
Carters Green 49
Coggeshall 37,43,47
Danbury 26
Doddinghurst 1
Eastwood 25
Elsenham 62,64
Farnham 66
Finchingfield 34
Foulness 5,20
Gaston Green 49
Great Stambridge 10
Great Wakering 6
Harlow 46,54,56,75
Harlowbury 48
Hatfield 47,67
Hazeleigh 40
High Easter 42
Hockley 18
Hullbridge 19
Ingatestone 3
Kelvedon Hatch 1,3
Latton 53
Leigh 16
Little Baddow 24
Little Hallingbury 60
Little Parndon 61
Maldon 15
Manuden 65
Maplin 20
Matching 50,51
Moreton 57
Mundon 31
Netteswell 55
Paglesham 11
Pleshey 44
Prittlewell 7
Purleigh 28,29
Rochford 7,8
Rowhedge 22
Saffron Walden 71,73
St Peter-ad-Murum 39
Salcott 32
Sheering 61,74
Steeple 17
Terling 34
Thaxted 59,69,70
Tillingham 39
Tollesbury 26
Tolleshunt D'Arcy 41
Ugley 62
Wendens Ambo 44
Wickford 4
Wivenhoe 22
Woodham Ferrers 13
Woodham Walter 33

BIBLIOGRAPHY

Addison, William - Essex Heyday. Dent, 1948
Bagley, William A - Essex walks for motorists. 2nd edition. Warne, 1982
Barham, Andrew - Lost parish churches of Essex. Ian Henry, 2000
Barrett, C R B. Essex: highways, byways, and waterways. Lawrence & Bullen, 1892
Beckett, Reginald A - Romantic Essex: pedestrian impressions, Dent, 1901
Benham, Hervey - Once upon a tide. Harrap, 1955
Finch, W R - Journeying into Essex. W R Finch, c.1950
Gordon, D I - The eastern counties (Regional history of the railways of Great Britain, v. 5). David & Charles, 1968
Holman, Gillian - Violeet Dix's trunk. Ian Henry, 1996
Jarvis, Stan - Essex. 3rd edition. Shire,1997
Marriage, John - Barging into Chelmsford: the Chelmer & Blackwater Navigation. 2nd edition. Ian Henry, 1997
Maxwell, Donald - A detective in Essex: landscape clues to an Essex of the past. Bodley Head, 1933
Morgan, Glyn - Secret Essex. Ian Henry, 1982
Morgan, Glyn - The romance of Essex inns. Letchworth Printers, 1964
Pevsner, Nikolaus - Essex (Buildings of England). 2nd edition, 1954
Pewsey, Lynn - A taste of Essex: food and recipes of Essex through the ages. Ian Henry, 1994
Pewsey, Stephen *and* Brooks, Andrew - East Saxon heritage. Sutton, 1993
Pluckwell, George - Smuggling villages of North East Essex. Ian Henry, 1986
Power, Eileen - Medieval people. Methuen, 1924
Quarrell, Johnnie - Portrait of Great Wakering. Ian Henry, 1996
Quarrell, Johnnie - Portrait of Foulness. Ian Henry, 1998
Roe, Fred. - Essex survivals, with special attention to Essex smugglers. Methuen, 1929
Rose, Stuart - An Essex dozen: a twelve-point progress from London to the coast, recorded in pictures by John O'Connor. Benham, 1953
Stow, John - The Chronicles of England. 1580
Thorne, James - Handbook to the environs of London. John Murray, 1876
Victoria County History of Essex, volume VIII: Chafford and Harlow Hundreds. VCH, 1983
White, Archie - Tideways and byways in Essex and Suffolk. Edward Arnold, 1948
Yearsley, Ian - Islands of Essex. 2nd edition. Ian Henry, 2000